ARIES HOROSCOPE 2015

Lisa Lazuli

Lisa Lazuli is the author of the amazon bestseller

HOROSCOPE 2014: ASTROLOGY and NUMEROLOGY HOROSCOPES

ABOUT THE AUTHOR

Lisa Lazuli studied astrology with the Faculty of Astrological Studies in London.

She has practised since 1999.

Lisa has been a regular guest on BBWM and BBC Shropshire talking about astrology and doing both horoscopes and live readings. She has also made guest appearances on Fox FM, BBC Cambridgeshire, BBC Northamptonshire, BBC Coventry and Warwickshire and US Internet Radio Shows including the Debra Clement Show.

Lisa wrote horoscopes for Asian Woman Magazine.

Now available:

TAURUS: Your Day, Your Decan, Your Sign

Includes 2015 Predictions.

The most REVEALING book on The Bull yet.

Lisa Lazuli is also the author of

The mystery/thrillers:

A Sealed Fate

Holly Leaves

Next of Sin

As well as:

Delicious, Nutritious Recipes for the Time and Cash Strapped

Paleo Diet: Get Started, Get Motivated, Feel Great

99 ACE Places to Promote Your Book

Pressure Cooking Reinvented.

You can find HOROSCOPE 2015 books for each sign on amazon.

FOREWARD

Dear Reader,

I hope my yearly horoscope for Aries will provide you with some insightful guidance during what is a very tricky time astrologically speaking with the heavy planets i.e. Pluto and Uranus at loggerheads in cardinal signs and Neptune in Pisces calling us all to get in touch with our spiritual side.

I have a conversational style of writing, please excuse any grammatical errors, I write much as I would speak.

As the song goes, "Nobody said it was easy." I know the mass media pump-out shows us plenty about quick fix love, money, fame and success; however, life is a journey filled with challenges and obstacles designed to encourage us to find out what we are made of and who we really are.

Embrace the good and bad and enjoy what is your unique experience.

Be the hero in your own personal life movie and never hide your spotlight.

I must add that the best astrology insights are gained from a unique chart based on your time, date, year and place of birth.

If you would like your natal chart calculated for FREE click on here:

http://lisalazuli.com/2014/06/30/would-you-like-to-know-where-all-your-planets-are-free-natal-chart/

Please join me on Facebook:

https://www.facebook.com/pages/Lisa-Lazuli-Astrologer/192000594298158?ref=hl

Contents

ARIES 2015 OVERVIEW

Aries are taking no prisoners in 2015. It would be fair to say that in the course of a lifetime, there will not be many years when the two biggest movers and shakers of the solar system namely Pluto and Uranus combine in stressful aspect with your Sun.

When we look about the world, we see unrest, turmoil and the breakdown of authority that was once trusted. Arians are agents of that change, but they also see that change reflected in their own lives. Arians feel the power and drive within to boot out the oppressors in their lives and to break down the barriers that are keeping them locked in a status quo that is far from fulfilling. Just as a chicken must break through its egg to begin life; Arians must break down whatever egg they are trapped in, in order to be born and to live again.

In the UK, Nigel Farage's (who is an Aries) UKIP party has caused a political earthquake by shaking up the three main parties – now you do not have to like him, support him or even know him, but the symbolism is right there: people are tired of a status quo that no longer delivers. Aries are tired of a lifestyle or job or relationship that is no longer part of their overall spiritual life path. Last year, Aries made many changes, and yet somehow the overall picture feels no different. This is a year of thinking deeply and understanding the key forces at work within your life that stop you being who you are or achieving as you should. Get to grip with the fundamental issues, the red lines issues in your life – should they be red lines? Should you have more red lines? Should some red lines be erased as you change as a person?

Forced this year to confront fears head on, you are going to be rediscovering that power of initiative that Aries possess and your ability to create something from nothing and go with it.

Interpersonal relationships are a key thing this year. Working with people and compromising over values and resources is an ongoing theme. Let's face it, Aries like to lead, but this year it's about teamwork and building something with someone else. You may be in a situation where you have to pool resources or even give up control of something you feel very personally connected to, to the group or partnership. You will need to learn how to get what you need from other people in a patient manner: relationships will have to be nurtured. When things are going wrong with your personal relationships at home and work, you need to be aware of your own traits being reflected via those you oppose. Things you may have wittingly or unwittingly done to others in the past may cause great problems in the relationship now. Be careful of who you confide in and who you voice your concerns to as allegiances are changing fast.

Another key feature of this year is role reversal i.e.: child becoming parent to the parent; husband becoming stay at home parent; taking over a company you always worked for. Somewhere in your life, a role will be reversed between you and some other person, and in most cases, this will mean much greater responsibility thrust upon you.

This can be a really productive year when you deal with the limitations in your life by either finding ingenious ways to get around them or crashing them out the way. Sometimes limitations are from others and sometimes they are mental barriers or things which we impose on ourselves consciously or unconsciously. Do not wake up one day at the end of someone else's life: look now at how to change your beliefs about what you can and cannot do and get rid of internal barriers. Then you need to remove the external barriers in terms of commitment and situations which hold you back from living your life.

Aries welcome change and so breaking negative patterns is simpler for you than for other signs as you are so in tune with yourself and so positive about life. Everyone has a right to their unique experience on this planet, and the drive this year to express yourself and get in touch with your core purpose and goals is extremely powerful.

Think with your heart and follow your heart; your heart knows your true calling, your head is conditioned to think about others first – which of course is needed in relationships, but should never lead to subservience and excessive people pleasing.

Disruptions to your plans this year or sudden events that cause changes in your life should be seen as opportunities to move towards something more positive and more in keeping with your long-term growth. Try and see unexpected events as pointers to where and what you should be doing.

Definitely a year to seize all opportunities and act with decisiveness. Do not look back; some bridges maybe be burned in 2015, but the only way is forward.

There are tests for your strength of character and your self-belief this year. If you know who you are and what you want then this should present less of a problem; however, any doubts about who you are and your ability to deal with certain events, career and relationship-wise, will be brought to the fore.

This will be a year where you will grow as a person and surprise yourself many a time as you discover hidden talents and also weaknesses. Your commitment to goals and your efforts to be yourself and follow your heart will be tested quite strongly. The main areas of opposition to your freedom and goals will come from authority figures, the government, financial constraints and change in the economy.

It may well be that many Arians in the light of pay freezes, layoffs, cutbacks, etc. are sparked into starting new careers or in using their talents to make more money from hobbies or opportunities online. You may leave a well-paid job to start up your own company. Within your work life; restrictions and constant opposition from superiors may force your hand. The change may happen quickly and be quite turbulent, but you will push through with determination.

An abundance of energy and ideas will carry you through this year. You are imbued with an optimism and faith in yourself that will withstand severe testing from others. Sure, others who have power over you can make this year hard, they can stand in your way. But Aries have their wits about them, and you will be able to communicate and think yourself out of corners.

You are very outgoing this year and more fiery than ever – this will help you tackle obstacles and have that oomph to fight your corner.

There will be some lavish parties to attend this year; you may even throw a big one yourself. You may be involved in a parade, a big religious festival, or in a big community event. If you are in the UK, perhaps it is the election you are involved in.

You are to excel in leadership this year: your ability to inspire and imbue others with confidence is a winning formula. You can tap into the social needs, frustrations and aspirations of the people you work with and really connect with people on that level, working to get better solutions.

This is a very powerful year for Aries to self-promote, and so if you need to sell yourself or sell a product or promote a new venture creativity, luck and originality will be on your side. Remember that the more your products or services are designed to help others or offer solutions to others, the more successful they can be. Offering services where you teach or offer guidance to people will also be successful. Selling hair and beauty products or even entertainment will also succeed as these things give people confidence and make people feel good.

For teachers and those who work with children, this is a really enjoyable year where you should see reward and achievement for those you tutor and teach.

Lack of discipline is a big drawback this year: yes, you have ideas and motivation, but dealing with admin, bureaucracy and keeping to a timeline may be far harder. This is why having a partner this year who is good with timekeeping, routines and dotting the i's is very beneficial.

Numbers and accounts are something you will have to get more to grips with this year – you really need to understand the financial side of your business and domestic life better. You may be making money, but you are also leaking it – have a thorough appraisal of where all your money goes, check your accounts and do bank reconciliations. This is where a partner who likes figures and bookkeeping can help.

You are warm and affectionate in relationships and will value stability and consistency from your partner. Quite a possessive side of you will reveal itself in relationships. Single Arians will look for commitment and for a relationship that settles down quickly.

It is warmth and sincerity rather than intellectual stimulation that turns you on this year. Single Aries may well meet a new love interest within an artistic environment, or love may blossom while you work with someone on an artistic project. Male Arians may fall for a woman educated in the fine arts. Shared interests in the arts and shared values in terms of enjoying peace and harmony will bring you together with someone special. Your tender side is very much in evidence in all relationships.

Highly romantic and sensual, it is very important for Arians that their partner be on the same page from the perspective of values and emotional reactions. More compromising and easy going than usual, Arians are putting a lot of effort into making even tough relationships work.

In same-sex relationships, bonding with someone special will take precedence over forming new friendships. In fact, strong bonds may develop suddenly without you expecting them to.

In all relationships, a degree of exclusivity will be demanded by Arians. Arians may even show a possessive streak, and they will demand many tangible displays of affection.

To a degree, Aries feel vulnerable in relationships and really need to hear feedback and reassurances that they are loved. While they are romantic, Aries are not always cuddly, but this year they will need more warmth and affection than usual, and if they don't get it in regular partnerships, they may become withdrawn. Single Arians will not be attracted to new partners who are not ready for something more serious or who are the type that tease and play games.

Intimacy may suffer due to the strains in other areas of the Arian's life, and so that is why a patient partner who wants to give loving a lot of time, not just a quick dip in, dip out, is so vital for the Ram's emotional well-being. Arians are actually very sexual this year, but they are enjoying it slow-cooker style rather than microwave and familiarity breeding content.

Your close and oldest friends will be very important to you this year, and you will confide in them many a time.

This is an extremely artistic year when Aries in the arts and entertainment world can produce brilliant work.

Arians are very driven this year and can work long and hard at what they want. They will make material gains and can have a great deal of success but must not neglect smaller details and the financial side of the projects. You are stubborn and need to explain your needs more to others both in a relationship and within your work environment. You are really good at leading teams and making wise decisions on long-term issues, but day-to-day you need to be more accurate in the way you deal with details, and you need to keep everyone in the loop.

Anger is an issue this year, and you must control your jealousy that can erupt for even vague reasons. You must deal with your anger issues that arise in an immediate and fair way before you jump to the wrong conclusion.

Single-minded at times, this is a year of great stamina and good physical health.

Older Arians must look after their hearts and watch high blood pressure and cholesterol. Stress is a key issue: sex and eating fresh food with less salt and sugar is a good way to deal with stress.

This is not a year where you will want to be alone or work alone. You will relish working with people and towards goals that matter to you all. You have a collective spirit, and as long as you have leadership and autonomy within the group, you will thrive.

This is very much a masculine year in terms of being a man, manning up to situations and all of those clichés about being a man. Your inner strength will be tested as will your belief in yourself and understanding of who you really are. It is testing and exciting and all part of a new chapter that began about three years ago.

You are on a drive to get things done – your New Year is off to an F1 style start. It is not just you; you want to place a spark into everyone you know and work with and infuse them with your own enthusiasm and sense of purpose. There is a danger that you may alienate others as you are too arrogant or domineering in the way you approach matters.

Avoid becoming so gung-ho that you become a law unto yourself: operating in isolation and ignoring good advice. Your impatience to see concrete changes emerging quickly could lead to you ignoring the finer points required to make these ventures and changes more successful.

You have not only the desire to start projects and make changes, you want to make changes within as well. You will research new diets, exercise regimes or lifestyles that will change how you feel about yourself. This is a great thing and will not peter out later in the year – what you initiate now will continue. A word of warning is that you should start slowly; if you have done minimal exercise in recent months, do not hit the treadmill like an athlete, and build up slowly to a level where you are comfortable. With exercise, like anything – too much of a good thing is bad.

It is not just your body you want to reform, you may look to hypnotism, acupuncture or even psychology to help you deal with issues you have battled with i.e. smoking, addictions, low self-worth and phobias.

This is a year when outside achievement is strived for, and internal achievement in terms of self-worth, self-love and more confidence is all addressed and improved.

LOVE

Self-understanding through love and relationship dynamics is the end result. In the beginning of this month, there is quite a bit of restlessness, and you will resent orders or limitations that your loved one seeks to impose on you. Freedom of expression and the freedom to act on impulse is what you need right now to feel alive and respond to the challenges you face – however, your partner may find you erratic and confusing, and may even doubt your fidelity.

There needs to be more give and take from both of you and some compromises to create more balance for you both – you cannot expect more freedom and understanding for yourself yet fail to give it back in equal measure.

Sexual gratification is very important this month, and so you need to iron out the domestic issues between you and your partner so that a wonderful potential for great sex is not lost. You want to be loved up in a magic bubble not sulking at opposite sides of the bed. Don't let small issues and arrogance drive a wedge between you this month – be spontaneous about lovemaking and let her/him feel your passion.

For single Arians, a hint of vulnerability hides a real animal this month – new relationships that are deeply spiritual and involving can develop quite quickly. Love liaisons this month will really help you get in touch with who you are, and even if they don't last, you will remain friends.

CAREER

Highly artistic and creative, you can do well in work or in your business this month by being 'out there' – go with your gut and use dreams as inspiration when it comes to artistic ideas or even when dealing with your boss.

Anything left field can come off for you as long as it does not arouse too much opposition from more conservative colleagues and employees. Be open to discussion and try and gently coerce those about you into your way of thinking – they are sure to come around.

You are thinking independently in your career; you are driven to challenge the status quo and find more innovative and more socially equitable ways of doing things. Office politics or the old school tie way of doing things will be a target for you as you aim to bring everyone around to the more modern and progressive way of doing things.

You may lock horns with authority within your work – you will fight for fairness and justice for your colleagues. There is a strong urge for reform and embracing new ways of thinking. If you can succeed, you will win much respect.

Strategy and vision are the keywords this month – see the vision, go with your gut, but plan the way forward in meticulous detail.

An insight into politics is vital to your strategy.

Things can be rather petty this month, and small things which you really know you should brush off will tend to niggle. You are struck by a tinge of insecurity, and thus any small thing will play into your paranoia about your ability to deal with things and people.

Misunderstandings, especially with your parents or those who have authority over you can cause some anxiety, and you will have to work hard to iron things out. Be clear and don't speak without thinking, which I know is hard for Aries.

Relationships with people of the same sex are especially rewarding this month: you may be a girl that gets on better with blokes or a real ladies' man – however, this month it is relationships with the same sex which are most rewarding.

Natural remedies and cures can have quite a dramatic impact on even long-term health issues – so whether it be eating more organic food, going Paleo or vegetarian, do give it a chance. Visit a nutritional or natural therapist to complement your medical care as a shift to a more natural diet could have amazing results.

LOVE

A very promising month for blossoming same-sex relationships. It is also a month when people who have questioned their sexuality may want to take things further in that vein – I did say this was a year of self-discovery, and sexuality is a big part of that journey for some people.

This month, you will gravitate to the person with whom you have the deepest spiritual connection: that may your partner, your mother or perhaps a friend. If it is your partner, then this bodes really well for both sex and love this month. However, sometimes our partner really does it for us on many levels but not spiritually, so he/she will need to understand that we have to go elsewhere for that.

If you are not getting spiritual nourishment from your lover or spouse, that does not mean the end of the relationship or that it is doomed, but it does mean that you need time spent with people who are on your spiritual wavelength, and your partner will have to get used to that.

In new relationships, you may be attracted or drawn to a new partner who you need to nurture or care for somehow – someone who is going through stuff and vulnerable. It is always a precarious position that of carer, do not abuse it or be abused either.

CAREER

A big case of back to the drawing board this month – you have all the ideas and the plans, but the finer points and details need thrashing out. I talked last month about strategy – you now have to refine this strategy in light of new info and problems that have arisen. It's not a major hitch, but a warning to get things better organised.

Do you have the right skills? Have you employed people with the right skills? Maybe you need to improve on your IT, language or legal knowledge in order to plan better. Perhaps you need some expert advice – don't be scared to ask for help and be ready to take a course or a class to get bang up to date in the field you are aiming to work or expand in.

There are loads of Google groups and hangouts, podcasts and webinars which can be taken in the evening or your spare time, and which can enable you to acquire knowledge and expertise fast, especially when it comes to marketing, social media, languages, business, health, etc.

In office situations, do not believe everything you hear; take a wait and see, approach and do not accept the grapevine gossip.

The solar eclipse this month will have a really big effect on you as it is happening in the last degree of Pisces just near the Aries Point.

This will create a boost of energy for you and herald new beginnings. You are becoming more aware of your potentials and how to actualise these abilities you have. It is also vital right now that you recognise your weaknesses and learn how to manage and minimise the way in which they hold you back. We all have weakness, and over-compensation can be just as much of a problem as the weakness itself – own that weakness and see it not as a weakness but as a trait that can sometimes have useful as well as un-useful consequences. Move away from self-criticism, and focus on what you have achieved, look at how you have got to where you are, and take that forward as you enter a new chapter.

This is a terrific month to move on and leave stuff that has affected you behind in the past. You may literally move, i.e. by moving home, school, office or job as the new moon heralds a whole new cycle beginning for Aries especially.

Put your energies into activities that contribute to your self-development and stay clear of things and people who bring you down. Self-doubt is self-defeating right now; be who you really are, the driven, energetic go getting, entrepreneurial Arian, who never gets down for long.

LOVE

The eclipse also heralds new starts to relationships; it is a very good time to meet people.

You will be meeting many new people this month and as these new folks enter your life, so will many prospective partners. Actual love may not blossom immediately, but there is a sense of excitement and anticipation within you and a readiness to put past bad experiences behind and give love a wholehearted try again.

In stable relationships, your partner will sense a spring in your step and a positive vibe, and this will enhance your love and romantic life. If the relationship has been going badly, or if your partner has been draining you emotionally or being difficult, this is the time to turn that around, and it is up to you to take the initiative. You have to set down some new boundaries, and you have to talk about how the relationship can change for the better. While talking does not always lead to anything in relationships as both parties tend to slip back into old ways soon, you are definitely ready for some changes, and your partner will feel that you are different. If you can communicate that well, then your partner will have to adapt.

There is great promise for a new chapter in all relationships

CAREER

You have no shortage of initiative this month. Your energy may lead you to lock horns with your boss or colleagues as you have a very clear idea of how things should be done.

Headstrong actions and impatience may not go down well, and so try to be mindful of this. This month is ideal for Arians who have a fair degree of independence or who work for themselves as they can take a few gambles and use that intuition to make quick decisions.

This month is ideal for tackling problems head on i.e. supplier problems, employee issues, client disputes. You are decisive, strong and very quick-thinking, and that will allow you an advantage in any negotiations or discussions.

If you are unemployed or not happy in your job, this month is THE month to do a CV blitz. Go for everything, go for that dream job that you think is unattainable. Whatever it is you want, go for it without reservations. The advice is to try out for a wide range of different careers/jobs as opportunity is the name of the game this month, and you never know what can happen.

This is an opportune month for getting to grips with your financial affairs. In the intro, I talked about how much financial issues to do with your work and domestically can be 'leaking', and now it is time to be more aware of how your money works. While this is also a good month to invest, I am thinking about managing outflows better. Look to find better deals for the services you pay for in business or at home. Stop doing things you could outsource for a smaller rate. Look at how you manage your time and see how you could be more productive by, for example, working more hours at home or by re-organising your routine.

Caring for someone you love is a theme this month; you may have to care for a father or someone who has been a father figure. This may link to a role-reversal I talked of in the intro – you may now be in the care or control of someone who once did the same for you.

Environmental issues are key this month – within your work, ensure you comply with all environmental health laws. You may actively participate in cleaning up an area or doing something to promote wildlife or protect a natural beauty spot.

LOVE

A very sociable month, where there will be many opportunities to meet prospective partners. Single or involved, all Arians should take the lead in love this month by spoiling your partner and taking the initiative in suggesting new things to do and places to go. Novelty and surprise are key ingredients for love and sex in April. Double dates and blind dates can work well and for couples a weekend away with another couple can be fun and relaxing.

Having children is a key feature in your close relationships: you may begin to talk about having another child, and if in a same-sex union, you may start to think strongly about adopting. The urge to mother and have a family is very strong. Sexually, a great time to start a family too.

You are very motivated by traditional values and yearnings right now, and that will impact on how you want your partner to behave. Try not to be domineering in relationships; you are feeling very strongly about things right now, and it is good to be passionate, but do not let passion become belligerence.

CAREER

Very independent-minded, you are sharp and strong when decisiveness is needed. You will be called upon to defend yourself verbally, and you will be readily able to debate. The ability to think quickly and make rapid decisions is key this month. Make sure you are not caught out by having a grasp of all the issues you need to. Make sure your paperwork is properly submitted and that you stay on message – do not allow a distraction to cause you to make a slip of the tongue. This is a month when an angry word at the wrong moment can come back to bite you; if in doubt hold your tongue. When angry count to ten before you fire off a response: this includes Twitter and email.

This is a very creative time for those of you who work in technical and mechanical spheres. Science and mechanical engineering students, researchers and workers can make great strides within their fields.

When defending your beliefs and ideas in the work environment, stay cool and professional, and do not take disagreement as a personal insult. For those of you in politics and law, this is a very favourable time for making arguments and debating; as long as you remember to listen and do not rush to the wrong conclusions.

A stressful, but productive, stimulating and challenging time at work. Expect changes, embrace them and make sure you adjust first to get an advantage. Remember Arians love to be first.

Life is less hectic this month and the changes it brings will be more easy to manage and far more enjoyable. This is still a time when work done and opportunities created need to be capitalised on, but you will begin to see fruits to your labours and reward in terms of profit and appreciation will role in.

Women will play a major role in your life, and they may have a great deal of influence over how you treat others, how diplomatic you are, and how you respect the rights of others.

It is a month of high passions, and you will devote time to the things that really matter to you. You may become impassioned about a new issue or devote more time to actively publicizing and promoting something you believe in.

LOVE

The middle of the month will be a tense time for relationships with sudden arguments and fall outs. Your partner may complain that you are too controlling and that he/she wants some time alone. You are best giving your loved one some space, do not force the issue. Take a few days to cool off and then listen to what he/she has to say. You may be coming on stronger than you think, and at times your partner may find you rather aggressive and bolshy in your manner. Your stress level mid-month is really high, and it is within relationships that this can cause havoc.

You will question each other's commitment and also debate issues of fairness in the relationship.

Your partner is especially sensitive right now, and if you are abrupt or careless with your words, life will be difficult. Arguments over the time you are spending at home, your commitment to home life and domestic spending may be bones of contention. It's not all your fault; your partner is feeling vulnerable and is behaving erratically right now at a time when you really need stability. The best thing is some space as this is highly emotional and cannot really be talked out.

For all Arians, there will be quite a bit of good sex at the end of the month.

Single Arians may look to make a casual relationship more serious or even propose later this month.

CAREER

You are very resourceful this month and able to come up with solutions to problems. With a great deal of mental energy, you will accomplish much. As a whole, you may not be very focused and you may lack direction – you will tend to do things as they crop up rather than creating the initiative. This is an ideal time to tie up the little details and create more organisation within your work environment.

If you work in journalism or media, you should be aware that a tendency to call it like it is and make comments that are rather insensitive could be your downfall – it will just not play well with your audience and could hit the wrong note. Of course, this can apply to any work position, be careful that when you are being outspoken you have the full facts and are still being fair. Everyone likes a straight talker, but if it comes across as rude or too caustic that can go down like a lead balloon. Dealing with transportation logistics or improving office communication and IT systems can be a theme.

Travelling in your local area or county/state to do business is likely. A great time to meet new trading partners. Avoid sarcasm with clients and people you do not know that well.

This is a very good month to start new projects or initiatives, especially if they involve creativity, promotion, sport or affect society in some way. Your ability to inspire and motivate is very strong as are your leadership skills.

Honour and prestige may result from your involvement in a creative or philanthropic enterprise. Selfishness and participation in projects for reasons of self-promotion or self-aggrandisement will result in the exact opposite of acclaim. The more devoted and passionate you are to a cause, the more effective and successful you will be this month.

Any involvement with children in terms of teaching, coaching or spiritual guidance will be rewarding and productive. This is a really good month for teachers helping children towards exams; for students taking exams and for sporting and competitive events.

A spirit of cooperation and working with people who share your values is really important; what is essential is not just achieving financial goals, but achieving ones that benefit humanity, as well.

LOVE

You are slightly withdrawn this month and are not communicating your opinions as well as you could. Your plan this month is the less said, the better and you are holding a lot in. You tend to be quieter due to some stress and worry over work.

Small things about your partner may annoy or depress you, and you may find that although these things are not unusual, they are more tiresome than usual, and you do not have the mental energy to deal with emotional dramas.

You need your space. Things will improve later in the month and events to do with your children will bring you together in a more fun and relaxed atmosphere.

It's a lonely month – your partner may not be as sympathetic to your needs as you require, and he/she is not picking up the subtle signs you are giving out that you just need a hug and some reassurance – don't be subtle. Just say, "Sorry, I'm stressed, I just need a glass of wine, a quiet night and a cuddle!"

CAREER

At this stage, your plans and ideas will be tested. Any financial plans submitted for a loan or project ideas, or promotional plans must be correct and checked thoroughly over. Due diligence is key for all work you undertake. Mistakes and oversights will come back to haunt you by resulting in rejection, disruption, and time delays.

If you engage in debate or are putting forward a proposal, check your facts are 100% robust and accurate. Do not cut corners. A few late nights this month mulling over details and paperwork submissions – this may be rather frustrating, but it is very necessary. Don't be shy to get a proofreader, lawyer or an accountant to check over relevant details, do not assume anything, make sure.

If you engage in international trade, insure your cargo and tie up international suppliers in contracts.

At no time this month allow beliefs either religious or spiritual to interfere with business judgement.

Self-control is an issue this month; you are not very disciplined – well, it is summer, and you have to let your hair down, but do not overdue it.

Not a great time for diets: you are inclined to over-indulge and take an *in for a penny in for a pound* approach, which you may regret later. On the upside, this is a very sociable and enjoyable month as long as excesses can be avoided. Don't run up the credit card either.

A certain lack of discrimination with the friends you hang out with or the company you keep this month may cause problems and arguments in your household – perhaps more with family members than with your spouse or partner.

You are trying to be all things to all people, and it is just not working out for you this month – you are over-stretched at work and things are hectic at home – don't try and be superman. Prioritise and if people do not like it, they had better get over it.

LOVE

After feeling rather lonely and detached emotionally last month, you are now totally back to yourself in terms of feeling loving, affectionate and demonstrative. You want to spoil and surprise your loved one – You've Got the Love in July.

There is one small snag, and that is emotional hypocrisy – in some cases you may be using excess effusiveness and charm to mask feelings and issues you do not feel you can deal with. Are you putting on a brave face? Is it a front? If not, and you are being totally honest with yourself, then go and have a ball this month. However, if there is something deeper nagging, don't lie to yourself about it, even if you are delaying dealing with it.

A great time for single Arians to meet new potential partners – you are filled with confidence and va va voom and being highly sociable will certainly attract lovers. You must ask yourself, however, what attracted you to this new person: their love or life, love of fun and generous giving nature or was it their lifestyle and social status? Often under these planetary influences we meet and are attracted to someone with wealth and prestige, but we are not attracted to the real person – it is a superficial attraction.

Look deeper into any new relationship and ask if there is a deep connection or just a passing attraction.

CAREER

Do not gamble on hunches this month; you may feel lucky, but do not allow that feeling to lull you into a complacency that everything will be OK – it may not be, and you could land up in over your head.

Be careful of promising more than you can deliver whether it be to clients or customers.

There is a head-heart battle within work this month, and you will find it very hard to keep emotions out of decisions. You may take an instant dislike to a new workmate or client, and it will be very hard for you to conceal that feeling of irritation for them. It is best to distance yourself from this person as much as possible – it is highly likely that your gut instincts about them are correct, but you may not be able to logically justify your feelings if required, so best to keep them to yourself.

This is a month when you should not tackle problems head on – skirt round them, avoid them and think long and hard before you finally deal with them. A delaying tactic could work very well.

This is a month of adjustments where you will separate yourself from people, places and situations which are not helping you emotionally or in terms of career.

Recognising and recommitting to duties and responsibilities is also a theme as you change modes of doing things and standards of behaviour that no longer match where you are going and what you are doing. It may be that you have now achieved a new position at work, a new job or a new client base, and you have to adapt to new mores and ways of doing things. It is a step up with a higher standard required and new rules and regulations to learn about.

Legal affairs and dealing with government departments are bound to arise, and so do keep paperwork in order and at hand and keep a note of dates and names of anyone relevant you spoke to.

It will not be possible to achieve or complete everything you aim to this month, as not only are events complex, but people you rely on will not perform as you expect, and there will be delays and problems, especially to do with legal issues and government.

LOVE

Mixed emotions will confuse you this month, and although you will look for advice, no one will really be able to tell you anything worthwhile. You feel restless and as if there is something wrong, but you cannot put your finger on it. You need to give yourself time: placing pressure and high expectations on yourself is part of your problem this month in all spheres of life.

Short-term relationships may break down as you discover that that person has disappointed you and failed to live up to your expectations and hopes. Maybe you have just realised that you and this person are too different, and the differences are not ones you can live with.

Clashes over day-to-day issues and how to deal with children are a common problem in marriages where there are kids. A stalemate is the best you can hope for right now. Look deeper: are you really arguing about day-to-day domestic and trivial issues, or is there something more fundamental that you are not saying?

Reaching common ground is a struggle in both new and old relationships: compromise and tolerance are the keywords.

Not a good month to start a romance as you are very confused and stressed.

CAREER

Within your work, it is important that you are up to date with all new laws and regulations that pertain to your industry. Be it health and safety, tax laws, emissions regulations, employment law, etc. you need to be well versed and to ensure that you, your business and your department are fulfilling the requirements.

It can be quite a confusing time within your work – you are unsure whether to expand or cut back as the economic signals do not make sense.

In an employee situation, you may feel unsure of what your boss expects of you: your role may not be well-defined, and you may find yourself juggling different priorities at work. It will be hard to keep everyone happy, and it is best to communicate this to HR and anyone concerned as it is not your fault.

Take time to work through plans and problems at work methodically and carefully as decisions and plans you make this month will have an important long-term effect

This month is highly significant in terms of the themes discussed in the introduction to this book. Your strength and energy will be tested as will most areas of your life. Things will reach breaking point, and you will have to make some decisions that will have an impact for many years to come. In many ways, once you have dealt with these issues it will be a huge relief. How you deal with them will require self-honesty and self-knowledge. The more you really know who you are and what you stand for, the easier it will be to make the decisions and be positive about moving forward.

Do not shy away from tough choices as unexpected events will force you to deal with them anyway. Events this month will test your belief in the course of action, career or lifestyle you have chosen, but by dealing with them, you can push through this and find new opportunities.

Underneath the confusion of this month is a strength and resilience that will surprise you. You are finding a side to yourself you never knew existed.

If your life has slipped into a rut, this month will throw up some unexpected events that will encourage you to embrace life again and start looking for potentials.

The universe demands that we keep learning and keep growing, and that is why it gives us challenges: it is not a punishment, but a wake-up call to opportunity, growth and self-awareness.

This is a highly-charged month: your ideals are clashing with real world challenges. You are both idealistic and practical at the same time. Exciting and stressful.

LOVE

Your general tension and nervousness, not to mention short temper and tendency to blurt things out can make all emotional relationships difficult.

There may be rows; silences and time spent apart. Aries have so much going on right now; they are caught in a hurricane of emotion, anxiety, ambition and self-discovery – this is hard on their partners, who need to be patient.

Aries are compassionate right now, but perhaps too busy to spend enough time communicating properly in relationships.

A stressful month in love – Arians must learn to find the cut-off switch and relax at home or else stress will envelope your whole life.

For religious couples: religious and spiritual pursuits are a great way to de-stress this month. For couples not inclined this way: theatre, comedy and movies can help bring you together, but only if they are not mainstream, but rather something totally out there and thought-provoking. Remember you are spiritually very open right now, and so the spiritual connection you have with your partner is the one you need to tap into … what do you both care about and believe in deeply? Reignite that passion for a belief, be it human rights, animal rights, God or food.

Couples that do not have a spiritual connection may split.

Arians may meet new partners via a religious or political activism.

CAREER

A month to be extremely strategic and play your cards close to your chest. Be very careful who you say what to – do not let your plans get out to competitors, and do not fully trust colleagues.

Being a little secretive rather than upfront (which is Aries default mode) is the way to deal with affairs at work. Do not be trusting, look for ulterior motives. Do not take anything at face value, and do not be drawn into plans/schemes that offer too much.

Where you work with or trade with people, make sure you know every inch of the contract. Being a Negative Nancy or a Suspicious Susan is not such a bad thing this month. Encounters with others will be fairly intense, and points of view both sides can become entrenched and attitudes hard to shift. It will be down to you to keep things going despite opposition from colleagues and third parties. Keep the vision in your head, find ways of pushing the obstacles and differences aside. Sometimes it pays to do some digging and look beyond the issues and obstacles and do some research on why: everything has an underlying issue; if you can get to that, you are better placed to deal with the issue or difference.

Look deeper; maybe you have more in common with those you are at loggerheads with than you think – do research, make changes, find common ground, and do not get stuck in stalemate.

A very exciting month of breakthroughs for those who work in science, medicine, engineering and cutting edge technologies. Keep going, you are almost there.

This is a month where things really begin to take shape. There is energy and the power to create and bring plans to fruition. In general, things will run smoothly.

To get the most out of this month you need to have everyone, either family or colleagues aboard. If you are trying to achieve as a one man band so you can claim all the glory, then this month's endeavour will not be as successful or rewarding. The more you work for the benefit of all concerned, the greater the end result, and the better you will feel.

A renewed communication with a sibling or an improved relationship with a sibling can be really important to you; especially in terms of the advice that person has to give you.

Legal situations to do with all matters can be resolved this month to your advantage as long as you have patience.

Make peace with your enemies and build bridges this month.

LOVE

Communication will be vastly improved, and you will have the power to choose the outcome in a relationship situation – use that power for the long term.

This month is a great time to talk about issues in your long-term relationships with your partner as the channels are open, and you will both be able to put emotions aside and have a rational discussion without arguing. You and your partner may unite over a home improvement or redecorating project or even landscaping your garden. You may also embark on a new healthier lifestyle initiative together. It is a back to basics, back to what is natural in the relationship.

This is a very good time for a single Arian to make the move on someone you fancy as you are sure to have success. Obsession is one downfall; take things slowly and do not let your emotions get the better of you to the extent that you become obsessed and lose perspective.

CAREER

Negotiation is a strong theme for this month, and you need to be very well prepared. Make sure you are right and have all the facts before you go ahead with any talks, and you cannot fail. Negotiations can be quite drawn out but will be constructive, and the outcome will be something you can work with.

In an employee situation, you may find yourself resolving a conflict or ongoing issue by being the arbitrator. Your diplomatic skills will be brought to the fore.

As an Aries you are forthright in all aspects of negotiation and will not go along with what you feel is not in you or your company's favour – your directness tempered with some diplomacy can be a real asset.

A great month to take the bull by the horns and re-organise your office or business to make it more efficient.

Your general restless nature is frustrated by routine and structure this month. You must look after your health this November and get plenty of quality sleep. Stay away from excesses of alcohol and sugary, fatty food, which I know can be hard as it is party season. While everyone seems to be frolicking away, you should not let your hair down too much.

You do have an urge to splash out both with spending and when it comes down to the boogy woogy end of year get-togethers, but the stars are saying BEWARE: do not max out your credit card or your body.

In all decisions this month, keep it simple and stick to your moral code – if it does not feel right to you, then don't go for it.

Realism and robust plans are the way to go about both work and everyday life – keep it uncomplicated. If anything you are involved in gets too complicated either from an emotional or financial perspective, pull out immediately and leave it to someone else.

Animals may play a very important part in your life this month: a new pet, rescuing a pet or looking after a friend's pet. Animals can bring a lot of pleasure to you and stress relief.

In diet, moderation is the key – you do not have to go cold turkey on anything that tastes nice, just know when to stop and keep the bad stuff for the weekend. Your system is stressed right now, and sugar, alcohol and additive-ridden processed foods will not help. Eat loads of fresh veggies, fish and chicken with fruits.

LOVE

In love, there is a spirit of compromise, even though there will be heated debates.

There is a build-up of sexual tension over this month until it all explodes with some really good sex at the end of the month. Arians may be a little too tense to experience really good intimacy with their partners, and you may both just be too exhausted really to put in an effort. However, later in the month, this will improve greatly with some very satisfying passion.

It is important for you and your loved one to have an awareness of how you are both feeling – make sure you communicate about emotional and sexual issues and not just day-to-day ones. Be more responsive and use your intuition. Often when we are very busy we stop tuning in to the silent signals our loved one is giving out, we become almost 6th sense deaf. Not all communication is verbal, and this month you need to improve your nonverbal interaction with your partner – fondling, touching, concern, sympathetic smiles, laughter, etc. Learn to get that intuition going between the two of you; this way communication is enhanced and those little sexual encounters each day will build into something more.

This month is a positive one for same-sex relationships that have recently started, they will develop into a far more fulfilling multi-spectrum relationship where friendship is at the heart.

For single Arians, a friend may become your new love interest in a very romantic yet sudden spell of dating.

CAREER

Within your work, there is an emphasis on training colleagues, new recruits or new employees. You need to pay attention to the systems within your workplace and ensure all the checks and balances work.

A higher standard is required right now in terms of the work you put out, and you may be scrutinised. Pay attention to detail. Large and long-term projects may be slowed down due to the level of detailed logistic or scientific detail required. A colleague off ill may leave your office overstretched, and you may have to chip in and learn quickly about a new field or department so that you can help out.

Sustainability issues may impact on your business – look for any government grants or opportunities for tax breaks as an incentive for being more environmental.

There are many opportunities for Arians who work in science, literary fields or academia this month, and it is also a highly productive one for Arians who do research in any sphere.

After a busy and challenging year, you will be pleased to know that it ends with a really happy, fun month.

Probably best to get as much work done before December gets going as you can as you may feel rather lazy and not very motivated (as far as work is concerned) to deal with mundane affairs.

You will feel light-hearted, and your ability to get on well with everyone is superb – time to put bad feelings in the past and take all relationships forward. There is a spirit of reconciliation in your chart, and you can be instrumental in bringing 'warring factions' within your family or friends together.

A favourable time to invest in art, jewellery or stocks and shares to do with retail or the entertainment industry. You are thinking very clearly and logically right now and can make a wise decision when it comes to planning financially for next year. You may begin to think ahead to a car you wish to buy or an extension for the home.

LOVE

Love interests that arise this month are mostly flings or possibly friends with benefits flings, which help you to cash into the spirit of the season without thinking about commitment.

The relationship with your partner is really great now, and there is a free flow of communication and love. There is a renewed sense of devotion and commitment to each other.

Christmas is really an important time to Aries, not because of the religious aspect necessarily, but because Aries love the tradition, the excitement, the decorations and lights, and the whole coming together of people really warms you inside.

You will be throwing yourself into festivities and showing your family how fully invested you are in them; it is a time for you to really show those who mean the most to you how important they are to you, and you will also receive the warmth you have craved all year.

Christmas Eve should be really good this year – sexy!

December is a real recharging of your batteries for 2016, which is set to be a very busy year full of big decisions, so you really can afford to take a mental breather from it all this month.

CAREER

A favourable time to invest in art, jewellery or sponsor the arts as part of your business.

You may benefit from a generous bonus from your company or a large gift from a client. It is certainly a time when hard work will be rewarded.

You may find yourself in a mentoring or advice-giving role to a junior colleague or employee – you are well placed to motivate, guide or even teach this person.

You may take the free time over the Christmas period to do some extra reading, research or learning to do with your job or career. As December draws to an end, you will begin to think ahead and start planning for the next year, and you may want to think about opportunities and new avenues to explore in terms of career prospects or where to take your business. It is essential that you take stock of socio-political trends and how those may affect your business and how you can take advantage of these rather than be caught out by them.

An improving economic climate should aid Aries next year in terms of pay prospects and finding work.

Some things may have been left uncertain at the end of November; however, from the end of December things will fall into place, and you will begin to see that the plans are well and truly working.

Thank you so much for purchasing my book – may 2016 be wonderful for you.

CPSIA information can be obtained at www.ICGtesting.com
Printed in the USA
LVOW11s1450120115

422492LV00002B/332/P